DISCOVER BIOLOGY

Animal Classification

BY EMMA HUDDLESTON

CONTENT CONSULTANT
LORENZO PRENDINI, PhD
CURATOR AND PROFESSOR
AMERICAN MUSEUM OF NATURAL HISTORY

Kids Core

An Imprint of Abdo Publishing
abdobooks.com

abdobooks.com

Printed in the United States of America, North Mankato, Minnesota
052021
092021

THIS BOOK CONTAINS
RECYCLED MATERIALS

Cover Photos: Shutterstock Images, foreground, background
Interior Photos: Jeroen Mikkers/Shutterstock Images, 4–5; Gil Wizen, 6; Shutterstock Images, 9, 16; iStockphoto, 10, 11, 12, 14–15, 17, 20, 22–23, 26; Abi Warner/iStockphoto, 18; Keith Szafranski/iStockphoto, 24; Rosa Jay/Shutterstock Images, 28

Editor: Marie Pearson
Series Designer: Katharine Hale

Library of Congress Control Number: 2020948367

Publisher's Cataloging-in-Publication Data

Names: Huddleston, Emma, author.
Title: Animal classification / by Emma Huddleston.
Description: Minneapolis, Minnesota : Abdo Publishing, 2022 | Series: Discover biology | Includes online resources and index.
Identifiers: ISBN 9781532195297 (lib. bdg.) | ISBN 9781098215606 (ebook)
Subjects: LCSH: Biology--Juvenile literature. | Animals--Classification--Juvenile literature. | Animal diversity--Juvenile literature. | Zoology--Juvenile literature.
Classification: DDC 590.12--dc23

CONTENTS

The splendid leaf frog has a yellow underbelly.

CHAPTER 1

The Animal Kingdom

Scientist Andrew Gray spent many years studying the splendid leaf frog in **captivity**. Its body was teal and green. Its underbelly was yellow. The frog lived in the wild in Central and South America. Gray took a trip to study it.

Sylvia's leaf frog was named after Andrew Gray's granddaughter.

But the frog Gray found in the wild was different. He compared it to science museum records. He realized that the frog he saw in the wild was the real splendid leaf frog. What he had been studying for years in captivity was a different **species**. No scientist had described it before. Gray named it Sylvia's leaf frog.

Classifying Animals

Scientists classify animals to understand how all living things are related. Classifying something means grouping it, naming it, and explaining how it differs from other things. The more unique characteristics animals share, the more closely related they are.

Other Ways to Group Animals

There are several ways to group animals. Animals can be grouped by what they eat. Some eat only plants. Others eat only meat. Still others eat both types of food. Animals can also be grouped by where they spend most of their lives. They may live mainly on land, in the air, or in the water.

There are several levels of animal classification. The broadest level is kingdom. Animals belong to the kingdom Animalia. Animals are living things made of multiple **cells**. Most animals can move on their own. Animals tend to eat other living things for energy. These features separate animals from living things such as plants or bacteria. Those have their own kingdoms. The main levels below kingdom are phylum, class, order, family, genus, and species. From phylum to species, each level gets more specific.

Studying similarities and differences among living things helps scientists understand how animals evolved. Evolution is a process of change that helps a species better survive.

Animal Kingdom Classification

Kingdom
Animalia

Phylum
Chordata

Class
Mammalia

Order
Perissodactyla

Family
Equidae

Genus
Equus

Species
— *Equus zebra*
(Mountain Zebra)

This diagram shows the levels of the animal classification system getting more specific.

Animals continue to evolve over generations.

Evolution happens over time. Classification can help scientists understand how living animals evolved from their **ancestors** that lived in the past. It can suggest which animals share a common ancestor.

The South American squirrel monkey is more closely related to other species in the same genus, such as the black squirrel monkey, than to species in the same class, such as foxes.

The world is full of animals, and each can be classified.

Learning how to classify animals is an adventure. Researchers continue to discover more creatures. Scientists keep learning how animals are related to one another!

Primary Source

Stephen Brusatte is a scientist based in Scotland. He explains how today's birds evolved from dinosaurs:

> A bird didn't just evolve from a *T. rex* overnight, but rather the classic features of birds evolved one by one.

Source: Emily Singer. "How Dinosaurs Shrank and Became Birds." *Scientific American*, 12 June 2015, scientificamerican.com. Accessed 22 June 2020.

What's the Big Idea?

Read this quote carefully. What is its main idea?

Mammals, including sea lions, have backbones.

CHAPTER 2

Phylum through Family

The animal kingdom is first broken down into phyla. Phyla is the plural of phylum. The animal kingdom has more than 30 phyla. The phylum Chordata is for humans and all vertebrate animals. Vertebrate animals have backbones.

Though crabs and insects live in different habitats, they share some similar characteristics.

There are a few animals without backbones in Chordata too. Many of the other phyla contain different types of worms.

The largest animal phylum is Arthropoda. It contains all insects, crabs, lobsters, spiders, and scorpions. Scientists have discovered more than

Birds are in the phylum Chordata.

1 million types of insects. Even more have yet to be discovered.

What Are the Animal Classes?

Phyla are further divided into classes. For example, within the phylum Chordata, mammals are in the class Mammalia. Amphibia contains amphibians. Aves is the class for birds. There are multiple fish classes.

Grasshoppers, like other insects, have an exoskeleton but no backbone.

Animals without backbones are known as invertebrates. They make up several classes. The class Arachnida contains spiders and scorpions. Hexapoda is the class for all six-legged insects. About 97 percent of animals, including grasshoppers and squids, are invertebrates.

Orders and Families

Orders are more specific groups within animal classes. Animals in an order share a common ancestor. The animal kingdom has hundreds of orders. There are 19 different orders in the class of mammals. Chiroptera is the order of bats. Rodentia is the order of rodents. Orders then break down into families.

Family Names

Sometimes suffixes show which level of classification a group belongs to. A suffix makes up the end of a word or name. The suffix "idae" is used for family groups. Canidae is the family of canines. Equidae is the family of equines. Ursidae is the family of bears.

Wolves are in the family Canidae along with dogs.

Animals in the same family share a common ancestor and a lot of traits. They often look somewhat similar to one another. The dog family is called Canidae. It includes 36 kinds of wolves, foxes, jackals, and more. They share features such as long legs, long snouts, and pointed ears.

Animals were first classified by just appearance. But technology has improved.

Scientists now also use **DNA** to tell how closely related animals are. DNA is located in cells. Cells are the smallest units of life. DNA is passed from parents to offspring. It is the reason living things look the way they do. Scientists also group members of an order based on shared characteristics. For example, rodents have teeth that never stop growing. Animals in the Carnivora order mainly eat meat.

Further Evidence

Look at the website below. Does it give any new evidence to support Chapter Two?

Classifying Animals

abdocorelibrary.com/animal -classification

Leopards and house cats are both part of the Felidae family.

CHAPTER 3

Genus and Species

Families are divided into genera. Genera is the plural of genus. Animals in a genus share many similarities and a common ancestor. The cat family includes several genera. *Felis* includes house cats. *Panthera* is for cats that roar, such as lions and tigers.

Animals of the same species mate to create new generations.

What Is a Species?

A species is both a level of classification and a specific kind of animal. Members of the same species are usually able to **mate** with each other in the wild and produce young. They continue the population of their species. They share many physical features and behaviors.

Each unique kind of animal is a species. It has a scientific name. The names are the same worldwide. They often come from Latin or

Greek words. The genus makes up the first half of the name. It is capitalized. The species is the second half of a name. It is lowercased. Both words are italicized. For example, the splendid leaf frog is *Cruziohyla calcarifer*. Sylvia's leaf frog is *Cruziohyla sylviae*. The frogs are in the same genus. They are closely related but still unique from each other.

Giraffe Subspecies

Giraffes were originally classified as one species that was divided into nine subgroups, called subspecies. All types can mate in the wild. But they have distinctly different horns, coat patterns, or other characteristics. In 2016, scientists studied giraffe DNA. They discovered that four different giraffe species actually exist.

Classification is one way to organize the huge
variety of animals in the world.

Animal classification uses many levels. Each one is more specific than the one above it. Closely related animals share more characteristics than unrelated species. Today, scientists are still finding new species and learning how to better classify animals!

Explore Online

Visit the website below. What new information did you learn about species that wasn't in Chapter Three?

Are There Different Human Species?

abdocorelibrary.com/animal -classification

Picture Biology

Kingdom
Animalia

Phylum
Chordata

Class
Mammalia

Order
Carnivora

Family
Canidae

Genus
Vulpes

Species
Vulpes zerda

Fennec Fox, Red Fox, Gray Wolf, Tiger, Plains Zebra, Red-and-Green Macaw, Green Iguana, Monarch Butterfly, Sea Star

Fennec Fox, Red Fox, Gray Wolf, Tiger, Plains Zebra, Red-and-Green Macaw, Green Iguana

Fennec Fox, Red Fox, Gray Wolf, Tiger, Plains Zebra

Fennec Fox, Red Fox, Gray Wolf, Tiger

Fennec Fox, Red Fox, Gray Wolf

Fennec Fox, Red Fox

Fennec Fox

Glossary

ancestors
past generations of family members

captivity
the state of living under human care rather than in the wild

cells
the smallest units of life

DNA
deoxyribonucleic acid, a tiny building block of life inside a cell; DNA contains information that affects the traits of a living thing, like how it looks and behaves

mate
to come together in order to have young

species
animals that look alike and, usually, can mate and have young together

Online Resources

To learn more about animal classification, visit our free resource websites below.

Visit **abdocorelibrary.com** or scan this QR code for free Common Core resources for teachers and students, including vetted activities, multimedia, and booklinks, for deeper subject comprehension.

Visit **abdobooklinks.com** or scan this QR code for free additional online weblinks for further learning. These links are routinely monitored and updated to provide the most current information available.

Learn More

Huddleston, Emma. *Genetics.* Abdo Publishing, 2022.

Murray, Julie. *Amphibians.* Abdo Publishing, 2019.

Woodward, John. *Animal!* DK, 2016.

Index

About the Author

Emma Huddleston lives in Minnesota with her husband. She enjoys writing books for young readers and staying active. She thinks animal classification is interesting, and sometimes she is surprised by which animals are related!